MICHIGAN
portrait of a state

MICHIGAN
portrait of a state

GRAPHIC ARTS BOOKS

The following photographers hold copyright to their images as indicated:
Claudia Adams/danitadelimont.com, pages 9, 11, 14, 15a, 15b, 15e, 27, 35, 38, 39a, 39b, 39c, 46,
56, 57, 65, 71, 76, 82, 86, 96, 100–101, 105, 110; **Ian Adams**, pages 62c, 62d, 80; **Howard Ande**, pages 60–61,
72–73, 74; **Thomas Buchkoe**, page 104; **Dennis Cox**, pages 17, 19, 20–21, 24, 26, 34, 64, 81, 84–85; **David R. Frazier**/
danitadelimont.com, pages 36–37, 97; **Darrell Gulin**, pages 15c, 15d, 23a; **Cheryl Hogue**, pages 1, 2, 22; **Adam Jones**/
danitadelimont.com, pages 16, 23b; **Steve Kaslowski**/danitadelimont.com, Back; **Ann and John Mahan**, pages 4–5,
8, 28–29, 63, 70, 78, 83, 108–9, 112; **Laurence Parent**, pages 10, 33, 44–45, 49, 55, 68, 77, 79, 111, Front Cover,
Back Cover; **James P. Rowan**, pages 6, 7, 12–13, 18, 25, 30, 31, 32, 40, 41, 42, 43, 47, 48, 52–53, 54, 58, 59,
62a, 62b, 66, 67, 75, 87, 88, 89, 90, 91, 92–93, 94a, 94b, 94c, 94d, 94e, 95, 98, 99, 102, 103, 106, 107;
Marji Silk, page 69; **Martin Vloet**/UM Photo Services, pages 50, 51.

Library of Congress Control Number: 2006926478
International Standard Book Number: 978-1-55868-988-6

Captions and book compilation © 2006 by
Graphic Arts Books, an imprint of
Graphic Arts Center Publishing Company
P.O. Box 10306, Portland, Oregon 97296-0306
503/226-2402; www.gacpc.com

The five-dot logo is a registered trademark of
Graphic Arts Center Publishing Company.

President: Charles M. Hopkins
Associate Publisher: Douglas A. Pfeiffer
Editorial Staff: Timothy W. Frew, Kathy Howard, Jean Bond-Slaughter
Production: Susan Dupere
Cover Design: Elizabeth Watson; Interior Design: Jean Andrews

Printed in China

FRONT COVER: ❂ The present Eagle Harbor Lighthouse,
situated near the point of the Keweenaw Peninsula, was built in 1871.
BACK COVER: ❂ The Pierce Stocking Covered Bridge, originally built in 1960, is part
of the 7.4-mile Pierce Stocking Scenic Drive in Sleeping Bear Dunes National Lakeshore.
◄◄ Tulips brighten the miniature Dutch village on Windmill Island, in Holland, Michigan.
◄ Miners Castle, at Pictured Rocks, changed forever when the fifteen-foot-tall northeast turret fell
in April 2006. Here we see it with the turret still intact, along with kayaks on Lake Superior.
► The ice- and snow-covered Upper Tahquamenon Falls have an otherworldly look.

▲ A flower garden enlivens a yard on Mackinac Island.
► A true living Victorian village, Mackinac Island has banned motorized
vehicles for more than a century. Instead, visitors enjoy biking, hiking, sailing, boating,
kayaking, and walking. They also travel by horseback and take horse-drawn
carriage tours. More than six hundred horses live on the island.

◄ Alder Falls plunges some thirty
feet over a rocky outcrop before continuing to
cascade over more rocks on its journey down the creek.
▲ A jewel of Hiawatha National Forest, Red Jack
Lake is edged by a colorful birch forest.

▲ Mosquito Falls, in the Pictured Rocks National
Lakeshore, consists of two main drops, the upper one about five
feet high, and the lower one about ten feet high, with a series of rapids in between.
▶ Near Rochester, trout lilies, *Erythronium americanum,* brighten the view.
▶▶ Munising Falls, just outside the quiet little city of Munising
in Michigan's Upper Peninsula, has a fifty-foot drop.

▲ A maple leaf adds color to a mushroom cluster in Hiawatha National Forest.

▶ CLOCKWISE FROM TOP LEFT: In spring, butterflies appear, including—

◖ A Baltimore Checkerspot, *Euphydryas phaeton;* wingspan, $2^3/_4$ inches;

◖ An Eastern Tiger Swallowtail, *Papilio glaucus;* wingspan, $6^1/_2$ inches;

◖ A Painted Lady, *Vanessa cardui;* wingspan, $2^7/_8$ inches;

◖ A Gulf Fritillary, *Agraulis vanillae;* wingspan, $3^3/_4$ inches; and

◖ An American Eastern Black Swallowtail, *Papilio polyxenes;* wingspan, $4^1/_4$ inches.

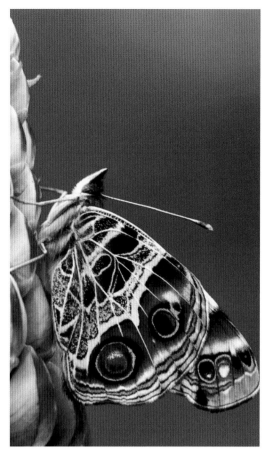

◄ Wild bergamot, *Monarda fistulosa*, dots a
meadow carpeted by black-eyed Susans, *Rudbeckia hirta*.
▲ Peterson's Mill, a working gristmill, is one of the
most-photographed locations in Saugatuck.

▲ A 4-4-0 steam engine, built in 1876 by Mason Machine
Works of Massachusetts, rests in Greenfield Village, Dearborn.
The 4-4-0, most commonly known as the American engine because so
many of them were manufactured here, was also popular in Great Britain.

▶ The five-mile-long Mackinac Bridge connects Mackinaw City with St. Ignace.

▶▶ Veldheer Tulip Farm is Holland's only tulip farm and perennial garden.

◄ Two white-tailed deer stand at alert in deep snow, in
Kensington Metro Park. The park encompasses nearly forty-five hundred acres,
including Kent Lake, a golf course, a nature center, beaches, and a paved hike-and-bike trail.
▲ LEFT TO RIGHT: ● A bird of prey, a saw-whet owl, *Aegolius acadicus*, looks for dinner.
Small mammals, other birds, frogs, and insects make up the diet of the saw-whet owl.
● A praying mantis, *Mantis religiosa*, does its "praying" on purple loosestrife, *Lythrum salicaria*. The praying mantis is also a preying carnivore, consuming other insects.

▲ The Detroit skyline rises above the Detroit
River, only about two and a half miles from Canada.
Traffic between Windsor, Ontario, and Detroit, Michigan, travels
on the Ambassador Bridge, as well as through a tunnel completed in 1930.
▶ The present Manistee North Pierhead Light on Lake Michigan was built in 1927,
replacing the first one built in 1871, and its replacement built in 1873.

▲ The International Bridge spans St. Mary's River,
carrying traffic between Sault Ste. Marie, Michigan, and
Sault Ste. Marie, Ontario. The bridge is 2.8 miles long in total.
▶ An oak leaf is decked out with icicles after an ice storm.
▶▶ Arch Rock, a natural limestone bridge on Mackinac
Island, soars 150 feet above the landscape.

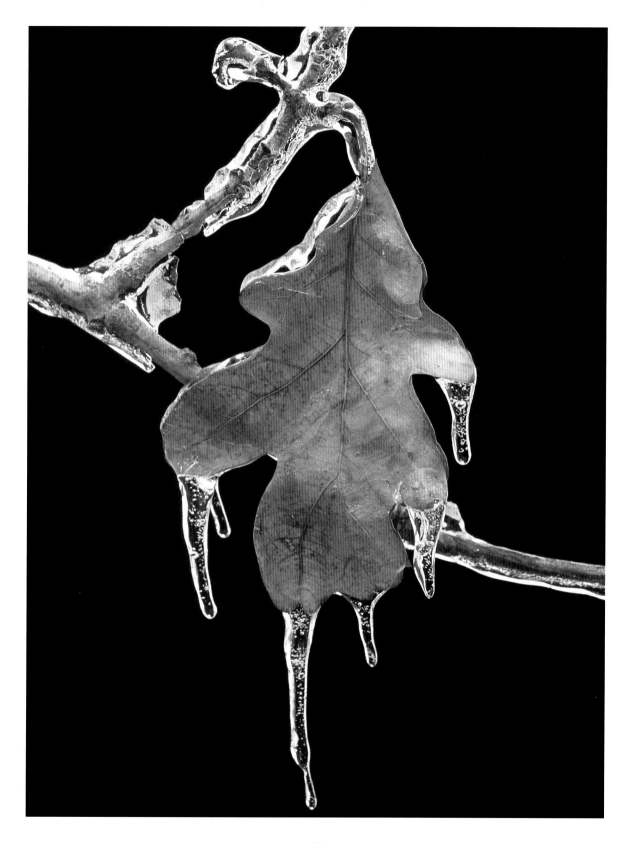

30

◄ Mackinac Island is home to numerous beautiful homes.
▲ The ore carrier *Stadacona* goes through the Soo Locks at Sault Ste. Marie.
The locks, first constructed in 1855, have been operated toll-free
by the U.S. Army Corps of Engineers since 1881.

▲ When the Heinz Company decided to
replace its headquarters building in Pittsburgh in
1954, the "Little House Where We Began" was disassembled
brick by brick and moved to Greenfield Village in Dearborn, Michigan.
It was reassembled there as part of a collection of historic buildings.

▲ Rapid River Falls Park, a park along the
Rapid River that features a four-tiered falls, includes
picnic tables, grills, and a playground.

▲ Bond Falls, in western Upper Peninsula,
is situated on the middle branch of the Ontonagon
River near Paulding. Its frozen winter aspect is unusually striking.
▶ A maple leaf decorates the ice at Bond Falls near Bruce Crossing.
▶▶ Situated just outside St. Ignace, Castle Rock rises nearly two
hundred feet above the surrounding area. Its pinnacle offers
excellent views of Mackinac Island and Lake Huron.

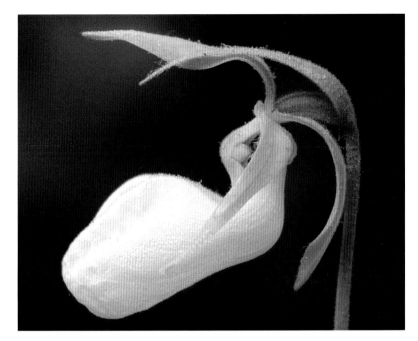

◄ Fringed polygala, *Polygala paucifolia*, and
dandelion, *Taraxacum officinale*, flourish at the base of a tree.
▲ Clockwise from top left: Wildflowers dot the landscape, including:
● A small blossom of White Lady Slipper, *Cypripedium candidum*, at Houghton Lake;
● Wood Lily, *Lilium philadelphicum*, and Harebells, *Campanula rotundifolia*, at St. Ignace; and
● Calypso orchids, *Calypso bulbosa*, in the Porcupine Mountains Wilderness State Park.

▲ The steamboat *Suwanee,* using the same
engines Henry Ford salvaged from the original
Suwanee in 1930, plies the waters of Suwanee
Lagoon at Greenfield Village, Dearborn.

▲ Maidenhair fern, *Adiantum pedatum,* offers a
lush green carpet in Hiawatha National Forest near Dukes
Experimental Forest. The national forest encompasses more than
880,000 acres of streams, rivers, shoreline, trees, wildlife, and
activities protected and controlled by the U.S. Forest Service.

▲ The Iron River Seventh-day Adventist church, built in 1937–38, is just one of some thirty churches in the town of Iron River, population about two thousand.

► Hume House, built between 1887 and 1889, was the home of Thomas Hume, business partner of Muskegon's most famous lumber baron, Charles H. Hackley. The Hackley and Hume Historic Site preserves the homes of both men.

►► Along the Black River, a forty-foot waterfall forms a mist—which creates a rainbow; hence the name, Rainbow Falls.

◄ The mineral-stained rock cliff and a pebble-
strewn shore of Lake Superior create new beauty because of
low water at Pictured Rocks National Lakeshore near Munising.
▲ The World War II submarine *Silversides* is retired at Great Lakes Naval
Memorial and Museum. *Silversides* went on fourteen patrols and is
the nation's most famous surviving World War II submarine.

▲ A 1931 Model A Ford Woody Wagon is on exhibit
at Greenfield Village, Dearborn. The Model A, manufactured
from 1928 through 1931, was the modern replacement for the older
Model T. Some nine hundred thousand Model A's still survive.

▲ Eagle Harbor is a rocky cove on
the Keweenaw Peninsula, along the shore
of Lake Superior. A lighthouse guards
the entrance to the harbor.

▲ Cheerleaders root for the home team at Aquinas College, Grand Rapids. Founded in
1886 by the Dominican Sisters of Grand Rapids, Aquinas is a Catholic coeducational college.
▶ TOP TO BOTTOM: The University of Michigan celebrates both athletic and academic prowess.
● Beginning in 1901, university sports teams have enjoyed numerous athletic victories.
● The Honors Convocation celebrates the highest levels of academic achievement.
▶▶ Situated between Norway and Wakefield, the Menominee River
is a highlight of the Piers Gorge Scenic Area.

▲ A Curtiss P-40N Warhawk (World War II) is just
one of dozens of aircraft on display at the Kalamazoo Air Zoo.
Other exhibits include a replica of the Wright Flyer and an F-18 Hornet.
► Port Sanilac, on the southwestern shore of Lake Huron, is a state-run harbor
and popular stopover for boats traveling along the Lake Huron coast.

◀ Snow-covered weeping willows
stand along a fence in Oakland County.
▲ Tree shadows create an intricate design
against fresh snow mounds in Deerton.

▲ Wright Brothers Home, now part of the Henry Ford
Museum in Greenfield Village, Dearborn, was once home
to Orville and Wilbur Wright in Dayton, Ohio. The brothers
built the wraparound porch of the Queen Anne-style home themselves.
► The brothers developed the first "flying machine" at the Cycle Company shop.
►► Neon lights up a street in "Greektown," Detroit.

◄ CLOCKWISE FROM TOP LEFT: Lighthouses are
common along Michigan's lakeshores. Examples include:
● The Sand Point Lighthouse, constructed in 1867 at Escanaba;
● The present Menominee North Pier Light, placed on the pier in 1927;
● The Little Sable Point Lighthouse, built in 1874 at Petite Pointe Au Sable; and
● The Pointe Aux Barques Lighthouse, built in 1857 at Pointe Aux Barques.
▲ Pictured Rocks National Lakeshore rises on the shores of Lake Superior.

▲ Grand Haven State Park is a forty-eight-acre
park consisting entirely of beach sand. Lake Michigan
forms the boundary on the west, while the Grand River
flows along the north side of the park. The Grand Haven Pier
and Lighthouse are a popular attraction in the park.
▶ Maple leaves in fall color brighten Hiawatha
National Forest near Munising.

◄ Founded in 1929 "to show how far and fast we
have come" in technological achievement, the Henry Ford
Museum in Dearborn displays cars, telephones, train engines,
and just about every other invention known to man.
▲ A beautiful fountain graces the garden of the
Grand Hotel on Mackinac Island.

67

▲ Miners Falls is a fifty-foot free fall at Pictured
Rocks National Lakeshore. Miners River was explored by
Englishman Alexander Henry, who searched for ore in the area
in 1771 and 1772. When his party saw discolored water oozing from
bedrock nearby, they named the river Miners River. However,
no valuable minerals have ever been found in the area.

▲ The Cranbrook Educational Community,
in Bloomfield Hills, reveals a peaceful campus. Cranbrook
is a center of education, science, and art—including a graduate
Academy of Art, contemporary Art Museum, Gardens, natural
history museum, and pre-K through 12 schools.

▲ Sturgeon Point Lighthouse on Lake Huron sits
aproximately halfway between the northern point of Saginaw
Bay and Thunder Bay Island. The lighthouse began operation in 1870.
▶ A frosty maple seedling has managed to take root in a pine tree near Wetmore.
▶▶ The U.S. Steel Corporation lights up the sky beyond
the 126-mile-long Rouge River.

◄ The Ford-Bacon House, built in 1898, was deeded
to the Wyandotte Board of Education in 1942 to be used as a
public library. It is now on the National Register of Historic Places.
▲ The Union Depot of Muskegon, built in 1895, served as a train depot
until 1970; in the 1990s it was deeded to the county. It now serves
as a convention and visitor center, bus stop, and museum.

▲ A skipper rests on a fern cluster, *Osmunda*, in
Wilderness State Park. The Natural and Wilderness
Areas of the park encompass more than seven thousand acres.
▶ In autumn, birch trees and sumac brighten the shores
of Lake Superior, the largest of the Great Lakes.

◄ Construction began on the original South Manitou
Island Lighthouse in 1839. By 1872, the entire structure had to
be replaced. Now a part of Sleeping Bear Dunes National Lakeshore,
the lighthouse is maintained by the Park Service as a historic structure.
▲ Potawatomi Falls, with a thirty-foot drop, is situated along
the Black River in Ottawa National Forest.

▲ Near Grand Rapids, a round barn is nearly hidden by trees
and shrubs. Because the colors are so similar, goldenrod, *Solidago,*
as seen here in the foreground, often provides camouflage for
insects such as golden soldier beetles and goldenrod spiders.

▲ At Chateau Chantal vineyards on the
Old Mission Peninsula, ice wine is produced some years.
Since ice wine is made from grapes frozen on the vine, and then
pressed while still frozen, it requires a cold snap at just
the right time to create this special wine.

▲ Near Port Huron, a purple trillium, *Trillium erectum,* blooms.
Purple trillium is also known by its common name of wake-robin.
▶ Windmill Island is a gorgeous oasis surrounded by the town of Holland,
encompassing thirty-six acres of colorful gardens, dikes, canals, and picnic areas.
▶▶ The town of Charlevoix's surrounding area includes pastoral scenery
and a jewel of a lake. Its year-round population of three thousand
swells to some thirty thousand during the tourist season.

◄ Wild columbine, *Aquilegia canadensis*,
flourishes with horsetail, *Equisetum*, in Michigan's
Upper Peninsula. The horsetail family is toxic, especially to horses.
▲ Yates Cider Mill, still a working mill situated in
Rochester Hills, was built in 1863.

▲ A fishing boat out of South
Haven plies the waters of Lake Michigan. Boaters
enjoy fishing for trout, salmon, and perch.

▲ Point Betsie Lighthouse is situated just
north of Frankfort near Sleeping Bear Dunes National
Lakeshore. Built in 1858 at a cost of $5,000, Point Betsie still
marks the southern entrance to the Manitou Passage,
though its light has been automated since 1983.

▲ A replica of Thomas Edison's original
Menlo Park, New Jersey, "invention factory" was
built in Greenfield Village, Dearborn, in 1929. Edison, whose
life spanned the years from 1847 to 1931, obtained 1,093
patents for such things as the electric lightbulb,
the phonograph, and the Dictaphone.

▲ A picture-perfect example of the proverbial "little red
schoolhouse," Glen Haven's Shetland School was built in 1871.
►► A reproduction of Luther Burbank's home was built
in 1933 at Greenfield Village. The original, situated
in Lancaster, Massachusetts, was the birthplace
of Luther Burbank (1849–1926).

▲ Clockwise from top left: Numerous exhibits
show historical military and Native American lifestyles—
• A powder magazine with a uniformed sentry, Fort Wayne;
• An infantry musician, ca. 1790s, Fort Michilimackinac State Park;
• Anishinabek nasaogan encampment, Fort Michilimackinac State Park;
• Anishinabek (Odawa) encampment, Fort Michilimackinac State Park; and
• A six-pound cannon overlooking Fort Mackinac State Park.

▲ Fort Michilimackinac was built about 1715 by
the French on the south shore of the Straits of Mackinac.
In 1761, after the French and Indian War, the French
relinquished Fort Michilimackinac to the British.

▲ A fly fisherman tries his luck
at Bond Falls, situated on the middle
branch of the Ontonagon River near Paulding.
▶ A fishing boat snugs in near pine trees in
Bay Mills, in the bay of Lake Superior.

◄ Grand Sable Dunes rise above Pictured Rocks National Lakeshore.

▲ A tree graveyard at Sleeping Bear Dunes National Lakeshore shows
how water and sand continually work to change the land.

►► The water just above Bond Falls takes on
fall colors at Bruce Crossing.

▲ Dune vegetation covers much of Sleeping Bear
Dunes at Sleeping Bear Dunes National Lakeshore.
▶ Remains of a shipwreck at Au Sable Point, near Munising,
highlight the dangers of sailing on the Great Lakes.

◄ A young boy celebrates his catch as he ice fishes
on a Michigan lake. Among the types of fish caught through the
ice are rainbow trout, brown trout, bluegill, black crappie, and yellow perch.
Ice fishing is a great family activity in winter, since all ages can participate. Some
people even build little huts on the ice to protect them from the weather.

▲ A snowy blue barn waits for warmer weather in the Rochester Hills.

▲ The Richart Wagon Shop, built in 1847 by brothers
Robert and William, now rests in Greenfield Village, Dearborn.
▶ This "tower" windmill from Cape Cod, originally constructed in
the mid-1600s, is believed to be the oldest windmill in the United States.
▶▶ Isle Royale National Park, in northwest Lake Superior, includes
Isle Royale and the surrounding waters and small islands.

▲ Fall foliage and birch reflected in Council Lake
create a colorful collage in the Hiawatha National Forest.
▶ The Hoist House ruin, part of the once-active Delaware Mine,
is incorporated in the Keweenaw National Historial Park. The
park preserves the history and heritage of copper mining.
▶▶ The St. Joseph North Pier Light, constructed in
1907, has been featured on a U.S. postage stamp.